W9-BKK-072

MAR -- 2009

You *and* Me TOGETHER

Moms, Dads, and Kids Around the World

by Barbara Kerley

with a note by Marian Wright Edelman, President, Children's Defense Fund

NATIONAL GEOGRAPHIC
WASHINGTON, D.C.

CHICAGO PUBLIC LIBRARY
SOUTH CHICAGO BRANCH
9055 S. HOUSTON AVE. 60617

Here we are, together.

Together, **ME AND YOU...**

Sharing a **JOKE**

SOC
R03260 39339
CHICAGO PUBLIC LIBRARY
SOUTH CHICAGO BRANCH
9055 S. HOUSTON AVE. 60617

Some **SHADE**

a **RIDE**

Playing a TUNE or two

Taking a **NAP**

a **WALK**

our time *together*, **ME AND YOU**

Holding a **HAND**

a **PET**

a **RAKE**

Telling a **TALE** or two

Making a **MESS**

a **MEAL**

a life *together*, **ME AND YOU**

Catching a **FISH**

NTE

a **BUS**

a **BALL**

Dancing a **TURN** or two

Seeing the **SUN**

a **STORM**

the world *together,* **ME AND YOU**

You and me together.

Forever. **ME AND YOU.**

Moms, dads, and kids around the **WORLD**

Arctic Ocean
NORTH AMERICA
Kidafell, Iceland
Chandos Lake, Ontario, Canada
Germantown, Maryland, U.S.A.
Antelope Canyon, Arizona, U.S.A.
Datil, New Mexico, U.S.A.
Staten Island, New York, U.S.A.
Atlantic Ocean
Piñones Beach, Puerto Rico, U.S.A.
Santiago, Guatemala
Pacific Ocean
Paramaribo, Suriname
SOUTH AMERICA
Canta Galo, Rio de Janeiro, Brazil
0 3,000 miles
0 4,000 kilometers
EUROPE
Berlin, Germany
near Rome, Italy
ASIA
Beijing, China
Kyoto, Japan
Paro Valley, Bhutan
Mumbai, Maharashtra, India
Jiddah, Saudi Arabia
Pune, India
Mae Hong Son Province, Thailand
Pacific Ocean
AFRICA
near Kampala, Uganda
Arusha, Tanzania
Goroka, Papua New Guinea
Bali, Indonesia
Indian Ocean
AUSTRALIA
Uluru National Park, Australia
ANTARCTICA

PIÑONES BEACH, PUERTO RICO, U.S.A.

Front cover: A boy takes flight with the help of his father. On this small, tropical island, many families enjoy spending time at the beach. PHOTOGRAPH BY DANA MENUSSI/GETTY IMAGES

STATEN ISLAND, NEW YORK, U.S.A.

Cooled by ocean breezes, a mother tickles her daughter as they romp together. Staten Island, just south of the Statue of Liberty, is home to many immigrant families. PHOTOGRAPH BY ANNE-MARIE WEBER/ GETTY IMAGES

KIDAFELL, ICELAND

Woolen sweaters warm two children and their mother as they ride near an icy stream. The Icelandic pony has been bred for over a thousand years to have a thick winter coat. PHOTOGRAPH BY DAVE G. HOUSER/CORBIS

DATIL, NEW MEXICO, U.S.A.

A father's lap makes a fine pillow for a tired cowboy. Cattle and sheep are raised on ranches across the state. PHOTOGRAPH BY NATIONAL GEOGRAPHIC PHOTOGRAPHER WILLIAM ALBERT ALLARD

JIDDAH, SAUDI ARABIA

Veiled for modesty, a mother plays with her daughters. Following Muslim custom, the girls may also wear a veil when they are older. PHOTOGRAPH BY NATIONAL GEOGRAPHIC PHOTOGRAPHER JODI COBB

BEIJING, CHINA

A shady spot is the perfect place for a father and son to learn a song. They practice in the park so they won't disturb their neighbors. A classical education in China includes the study of music, board games, calligraphy, and painting. PHOTOGRAPH BY STUART FRANKLIN/MAGNUM PHOTOS

MAE HONG SON PROVINCE, THAILAND

A Padaung mother strums a wooden guitar for her daughter. Traditionally, girls begin to wear brass neck rings when they are five or six years old. PHOTOGRAPH BY CHRIS LISLE/CORBIS

PARO VALLEY, BHUTAN

A son's good company lightens his mother's heavy load. In Bhutan, goods such as firewood and hay may be transported on foot. PHOTOGRAPH BY R. IAN LLOYD/MASTERFILE

KYOTO, JAPAN

Wearing a traditional hairpiece and clothing, a girl holds her mother's hand. They will celebrate the Festival of Ages, which honors the more than thousand years Kyoto served as Japan's capital. Their costumes reflect the city's rich and varied history. PHOTOGRAPH BY LINC CORNELL/INDEX STOCK

ARUSHA, TANZANIA

In the shadow of Longido Mountain, a boy stands next to his father, holding a pet goat. Raising livestock—cattle, sheep, and goats—is an important part of Maasai culture. PHOTOGRAPH BY ALISON WRIGHT/CORBIS

BALI, INDONESIA

A father and son carry rakes as they walk through a rice field. Much of the work of growing rice, a staple crop in Southeast Asia, is done by hand. PHOTOGRAPH BY JACK FIELDS/CORBIS

SANTIAGO, GUATEMALA

A father and son swap stories on a sunny day. Maya culture includes a rich tradition of storytelling. PHOTOGRAPH BY FRANS LEMMENS/GETTY IMAGES

PUNE, INDIA

A mother and daughter cover each other with colored powder for Holi festival. Celebrating the arrival of spring, Holi is a time to make colorful messes, visit friends, and eat sweets. PHOTOGRAPH COURTESY OF CORBIS

NEAR ROME, ITALY

Two girls wait patiently for their mother to finish cooking. For Gypsy, or Roma, families who are traditionally on the move, a kitchen can be anyplace with a good, hot fire. PHOTOGRAPH BY DAVID TURNLEY/CORBIS

CANTA GALO, RIO DE JANEIRO, BRAZIL

A father and son enjoy an afternoon of fishing on a quiet lake. The fish they catch may be prepared with tomatoes, peppers, and coconut milk in a dish called *moqueca.* PHOTOGRAPH BY SILVESTRE MACHADO/GETTY IMAGES

BERLIN, GERMANY

Wearing a bright red hat for the outing, a daughter smiles with her father as they watch the world pass by. PHOTOGRAPH BY GEOFFREY CLIFFORD/GETTY IMAGES

NEAR KAMPALA, UGANDA

Reaching high overhead, children toss a ball with their mother. Although ill with AIDS, their mother enjoys playing ball with her children. PHOTOGRAPH BY LOUISE GUBB/CORBIS SABA

GERMANTOWN, MARYLAND, U.S.A.

A daughter's toes are safe when she stands atop her father's big, black shoes. The waltz, popular in Europe during the 19th Century, is still enjoyed today. PHOTOGRAPH BY DANIEL R. WESTERGREN, NATIONAL GEOGRAPHIC SOCIETY

ANTELOPE CANYON, ARIZONA, U.S.A.

A mother and daughter find a shaft of sunlight through the red-rock walls of a slot canyon. Cut into the sandstone bedrock by centuries of wind and rain, the canyon is in some spots only three feet wide. PHOTOGRAPH BY PAUL DAMIEN/NGS IMAGE COLLECTION

MUMBAI, MAHARASHTRA, INDIA

Monsoon rains wash over a mother and her daughter as they walk together. Based on the Arabic word *mawsim,* this "season" of winds brings rainy weather to much of South Asia. PHOTOGRAPH BY JAGDISH AGARWAL/SCPHOTOS/ALAMY IMAGES

CHANDOS LAKE, ONTARIO, CANADA

A father and son paddle a canoe at day's end. PHOTOGRAPH BY PETER GRIFFITH/MASTERFILE

PARAMARIBO, SURINAME

A daughter joins her mother in celebrating the holiday of Eid al Fitr. After the month-long fast of Ramadan, Muslim families around the world enjoy this day of feasting. PHOTOGRAPH BY ROBERT CAPUTO/AURORA

GOROKA, PAPUA NEW GUINEA

Asaro fathers and sons, made up as "Mudmen," come together for the annual sing-sing. Families from all over the country meet to share tribal songs and dances. PHOTOGRAPH BY NATIONAL GEOGRAPHIC PHOTOGRAPHER JODI COBB

ULURU NATIONAL PARK, AUSTRALIA

Back cover: Watching his father carefully, an Aborigine son learns how to carve a boomerang. Once completed, it can be used in ceremonies or for hunting. PHOTOGRAPH BY RICHARD T. NOWITZ/CORBIS

A note on *the world's* **CHILDREN**

Parents love their children, and children love their parents. As this magical collection of photographs and words makes abundantly clear, parents and children find joy in each other day in and day out, over meals and at play, sharing work, making music, while dancing and praying—or just being together. Love between parents and children is universal, and we see it shining here from Tanzania to Germany, from Bhutan to New Mexico. Our children are precious. But for many children of this world, love alone does not sustain them. Worse, for some children of this world, love is not even familiar.

> **CHILDREN** are *one third* of our population and *all* of our **FUTURE.**
>
> —Select Panel for the Promotion of Child Health

Yes, parents love their children, but we need a world of parents who love *all* children. We need parents who will not just take the hand of their own child but will offer a helping hand to a community and nation of children. We need parents who will not just read to a daughter before bedtime but who will raise insistent voices for education for a generation of girls in places where learning is lacking or saved only for boys. We need parents who will not just listen to the dreams of a single son but who will realize the right of every child with whom that son must share a world to pursue a dream.

Why have we endangered so badly the hopes and lives of so many children? What kind of world permits 38,000 children to die every day from preventable poverty-related causes? What kind of world lets children and mothers die in violent wars

CELEBRATING TOGETHER: *A daughter joins her mother in prayer on the Muslim holiday of Eid al Fitr. Children begin learning the customs and cultures of their countries from their parents.*